THIS EASTER ACTIVITY BOOK BELONGS TO MY FANTASTIC FRIEND:

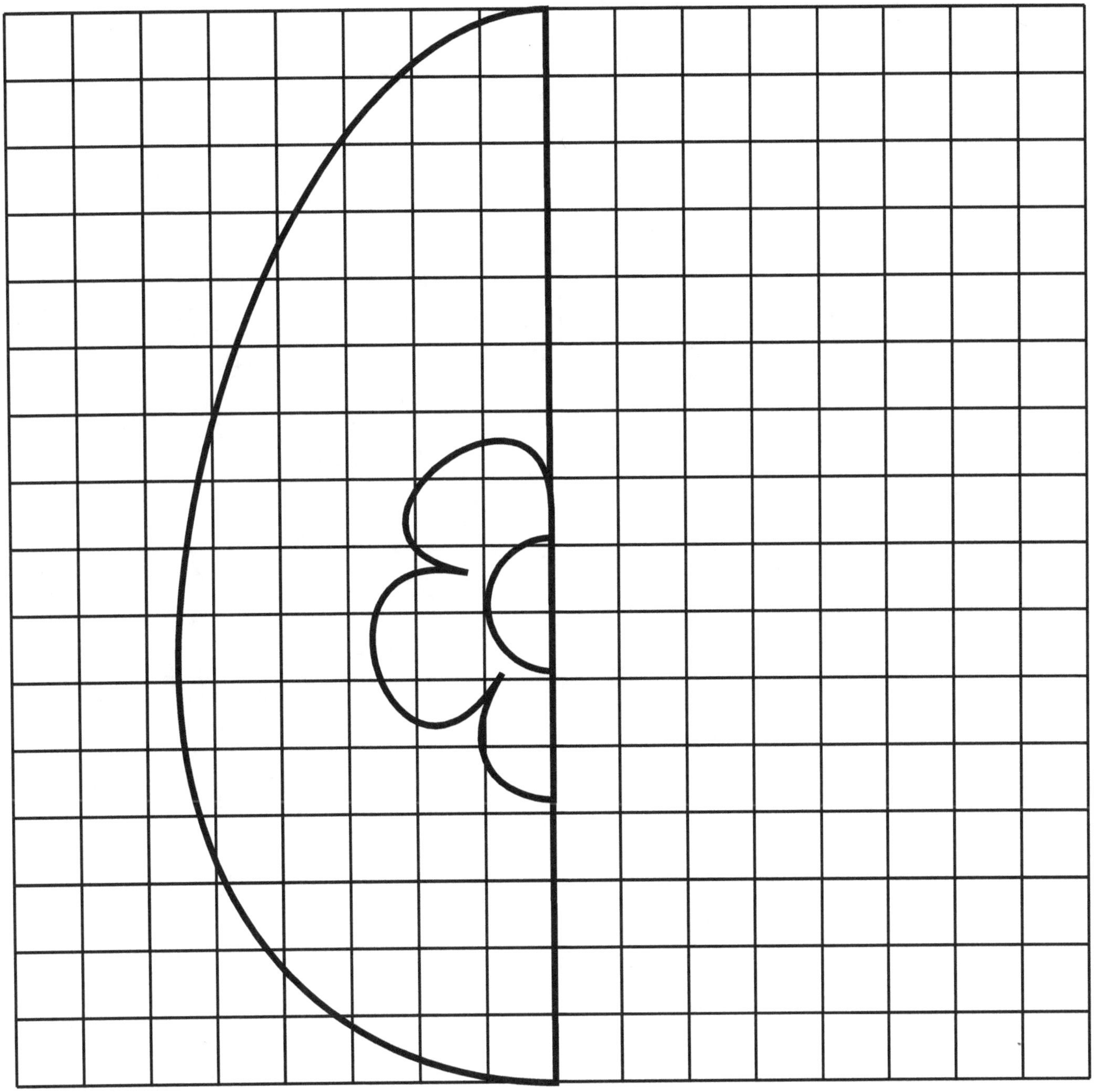

USE THE GRID TO DRAW & COLOR THE EASTER EGG.

Color and name all of the season of the year.

ANIMAL WORD SEARCH FOR MY FRIEND!
Find these animals:
rabbit
bear
elephant
hamster

a	c	o	w	p	d	v	h	f	i
m	n	o	p	q	r	s	t	j	v
f	h	g	z	k	y	x	w	x	u
c	b	p	e	n	g	u	i	n	p
a	i	j	m	f	z	y	x	z	t
d	b	d	o	b	k	m	p	t	y
g	f	i	n	j	m	z	y	i	w
e	d	z	k	i	l	o	p	g	x
f	h	j	e	e	m	w	l	e	t
e	m	h	y	l	o	p	q	r	w

Draw and color a picture of the LAMB using the grid.

Complete the maze and color the CHICK.

A FANTASTIC FRIEND'S LITTLE BUNNY
DRAW & COLOR GRID

Draw the other half of the bunny using the grid and then color the BUNNY.

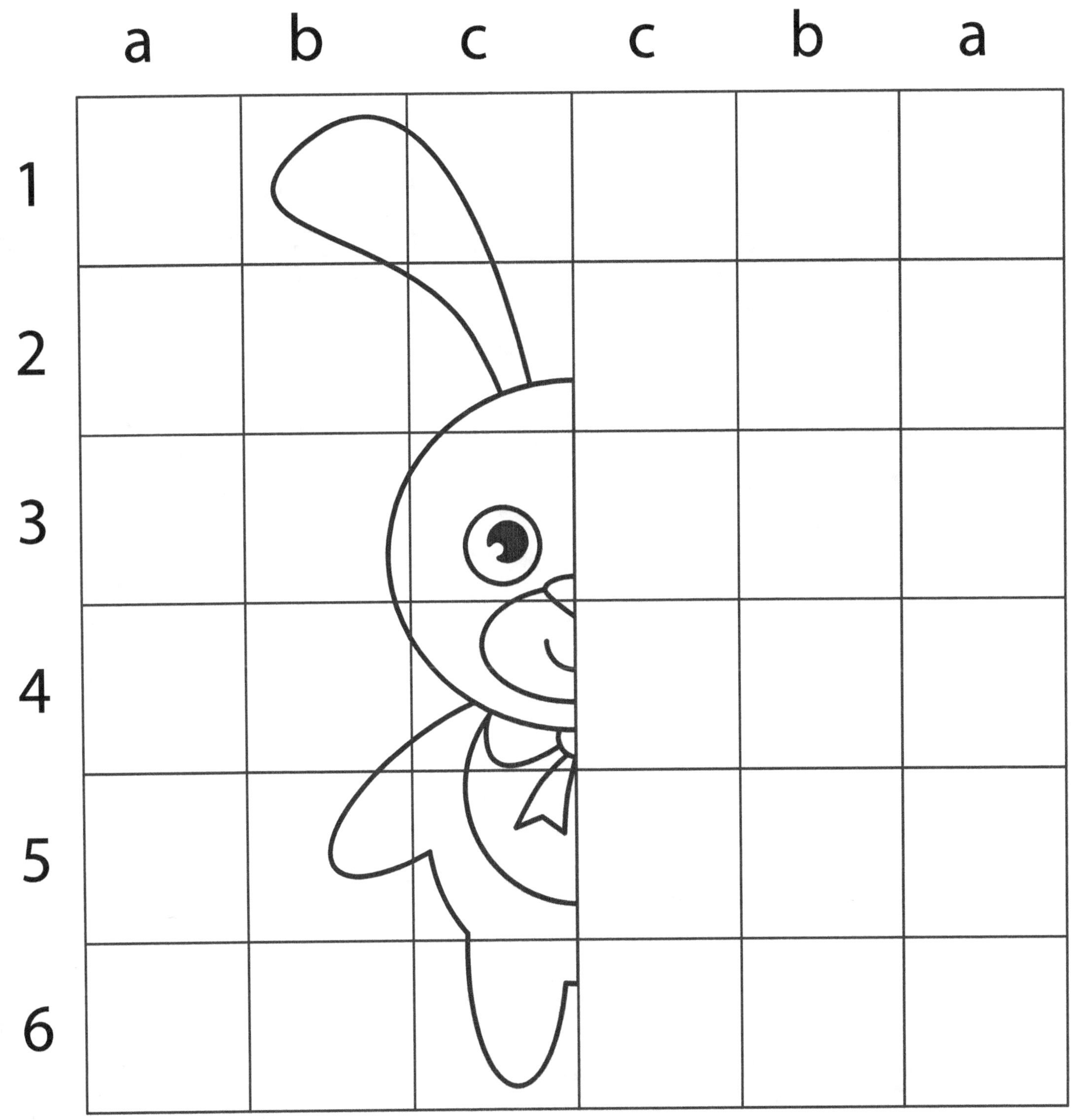

JELLY BEAN POEM

J is for jelly beans.
Red, green, or blue.
Jelly beans for me.
Jelly beans for you.
5, 10, 15, 20, 25, or more,
I like to count jelly beans,
1, 2, 3, 4!

By Tracy Piltz

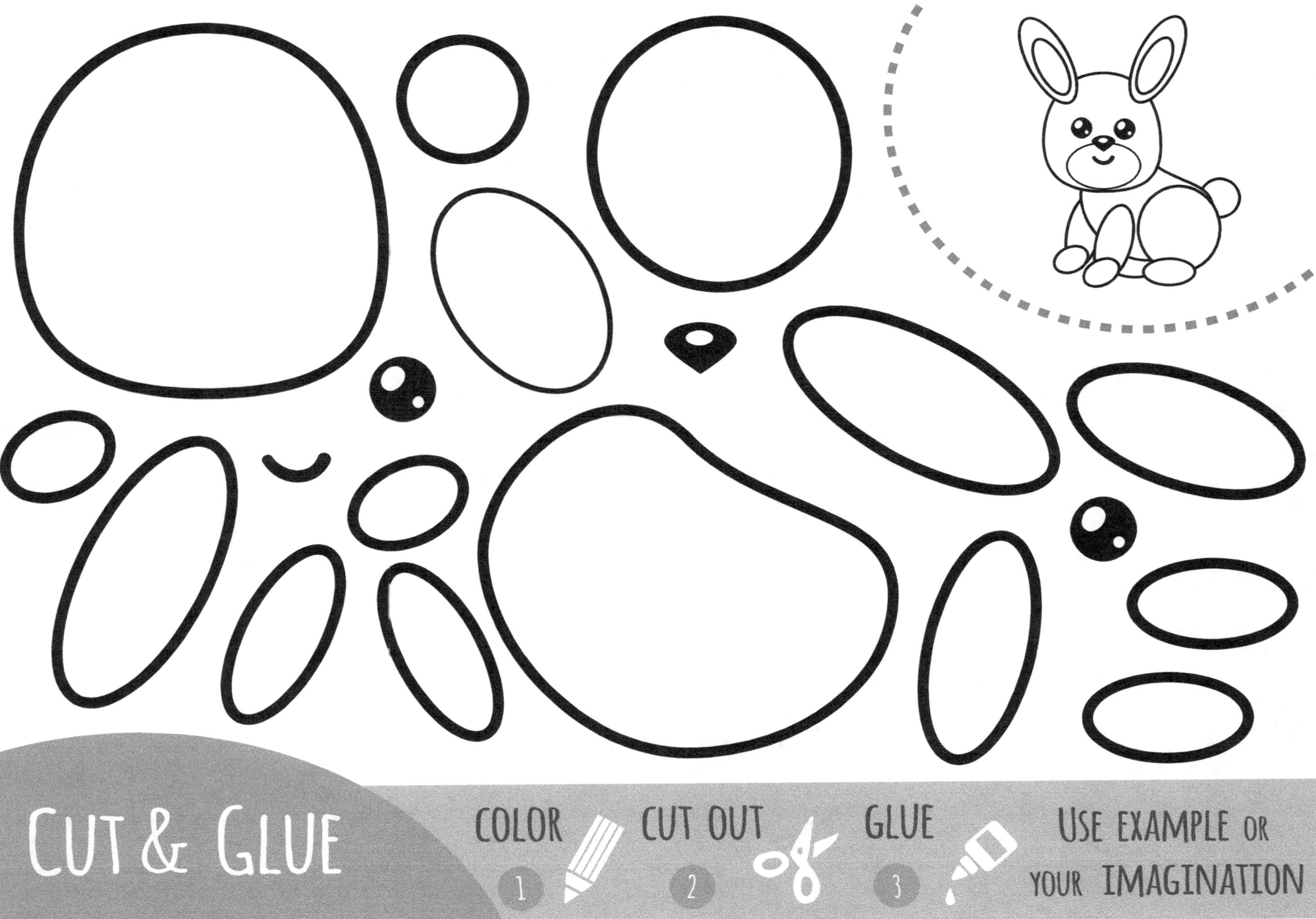
Cut & Glue
COLOR
CUT OUT
GLUE
USE EXAMPLE OR YOUR IMAGINATION
1
2
3

Cut & Glue
COLOR
CUT OUT
GLUE
1
2
3
USE EXAMPLE OR YOUR IMAGINATION

SPRING MAZE FOR A FANTASTIC FRIEND!

Complete the maze to help BUNNY reach the carrots. Then help the LADY BUG reach the flowers and color all of the spring objects.

CHICK DOT-TO-DOT
Connect the dots (from 1-26) and color the CHICK.

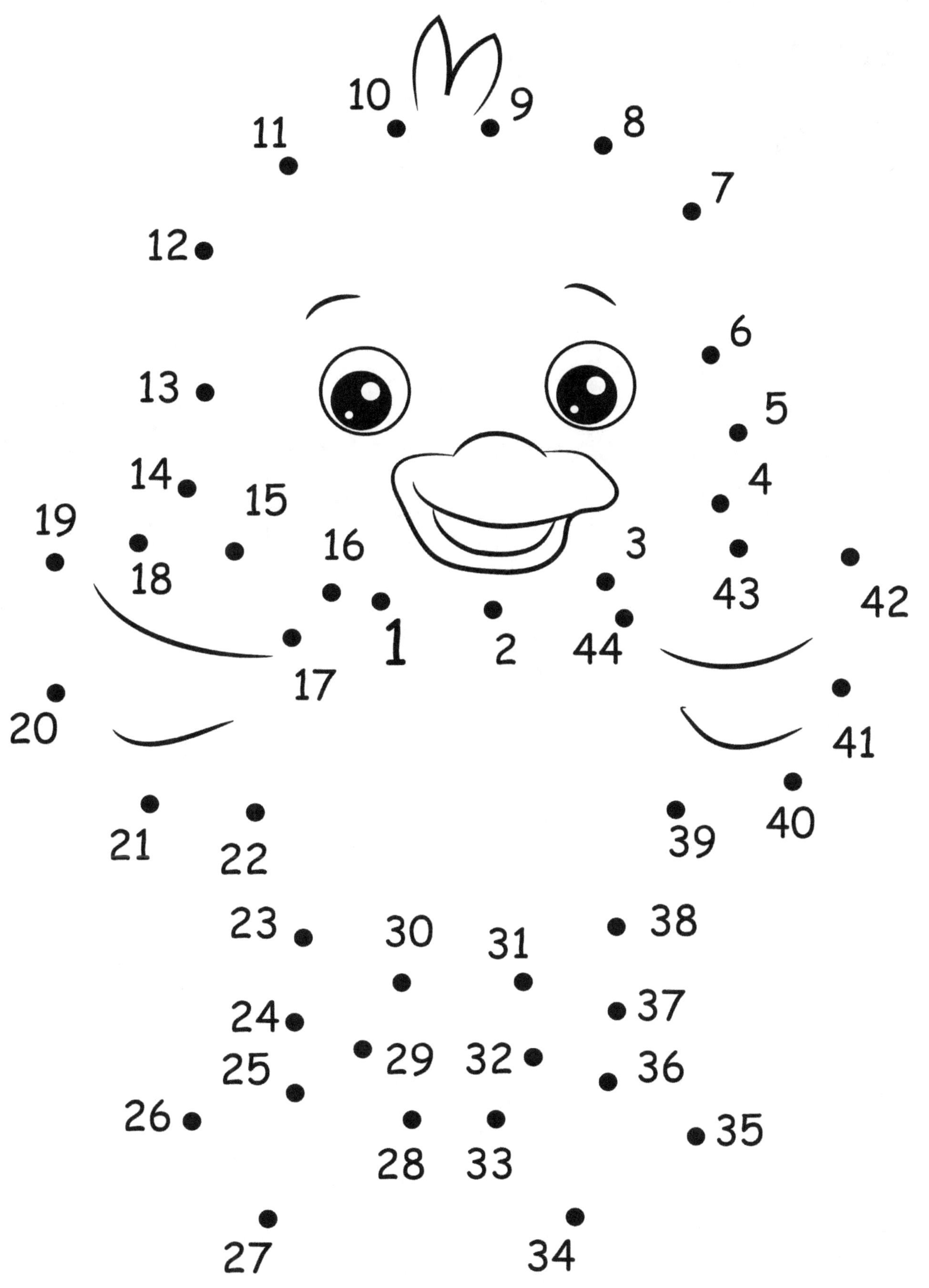

I'M A LITTLE BUNNY
(Song from the tune of: I'm a little teapot)

I'M A LITTLE BUNNY
WITH A COTTON TAIL,
SEE ME HOPPING
DOWN THE TRAIL,
WHEN I SEE CARROTS,
MY EARS, THEY SHAKE!
AND THEN, OF COURSE,
A BITE I TAKE!
CRUNCH!!!!

SHEEP DOT-TO-DOT
Complete the maze and color the SHEEP.

I'M AN EASTER BUNNY

I'm an Easter bunny, watch me hop
(hop around).

Here are my two ears, see how they flop
(hold hand at sides of head & flop them).

Here is my cotton tail, here is my nose
(wiggle hips, then point to nose).

I'm all furry, from my head to my toes
(point to head then to toes).
By Susan Paprocki

FRIEND,
Can you help the
chicken catch the
rabbits?

BUNNY DOT-TO-DOT
Connect the dots (from 1-26) and then color the BUNNY.

ANIMALS IN THE BARNYARD FOR MY FANTASTIC FRIEND!

Count and write the number of each animal in the box (BULL, HORSE, PIG, AND SHEEP). What is the total number of animals on the page?

FUN RABBIT MAZES!
Complete the mazes and then color the rabbits & eggs.

AN EASTER EGG FOR MY FANTASTIC FRIEND!

Connect the dots and then color the beautiful EASTER EGG.

EASTER BUNNY POEM
The Easter bunny's feet
Go hop, hop, hop,
While their big pink ears
Go flop, flop, flop,
They are rushing on their way
To bring us eggs on Easter Day,
With a hop, flop, hop, flop, hop!!!

BUNNY FUN DOT-TO-DOT
Connect the dots (from 1-26) and then color the
BUNNIES.

CUT & GLUE
COLOR
1
CUT OUT
2
GLUE
3
USE EXAMPLE OR YOUR IMAGINATION

CUT & GLUE
COLOR
1
CUT OUT
2
GLUE
3
USE EXAMPLE OR YOUR IMAGINATION

AN EASTER BASKET FOR MY FRIEND!
Connect the dots and color the EASTER BASKET.

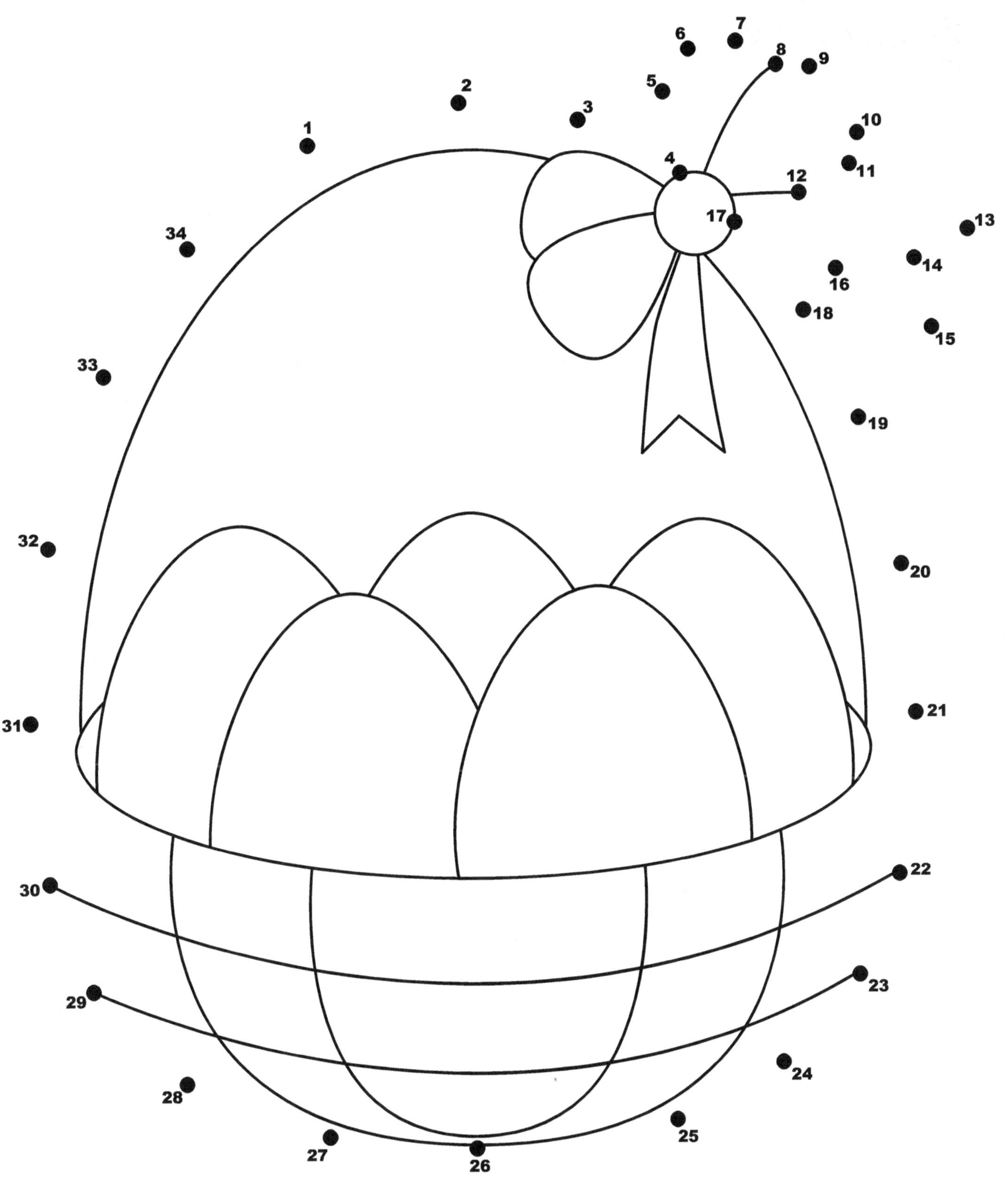

Draw and color a picture of the EASTER BUNNY using the grid.

EGG-CITING EGG MAZE
Complete the maze and color the EGG.

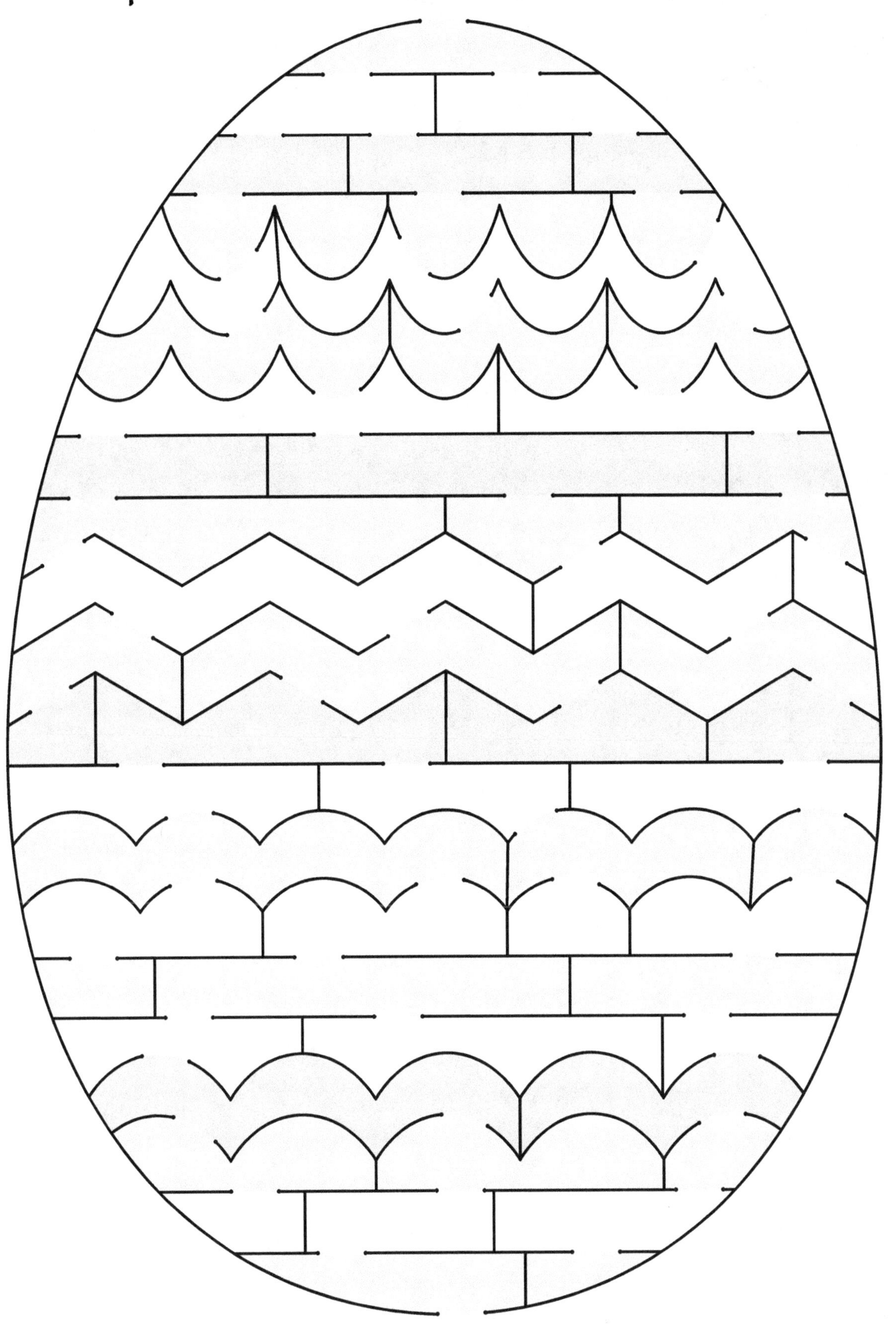

COLOR BY NUMBER:

1-light blue

2-dark pink

3-light green

4-dark green

5-gray

6-orange

7- red

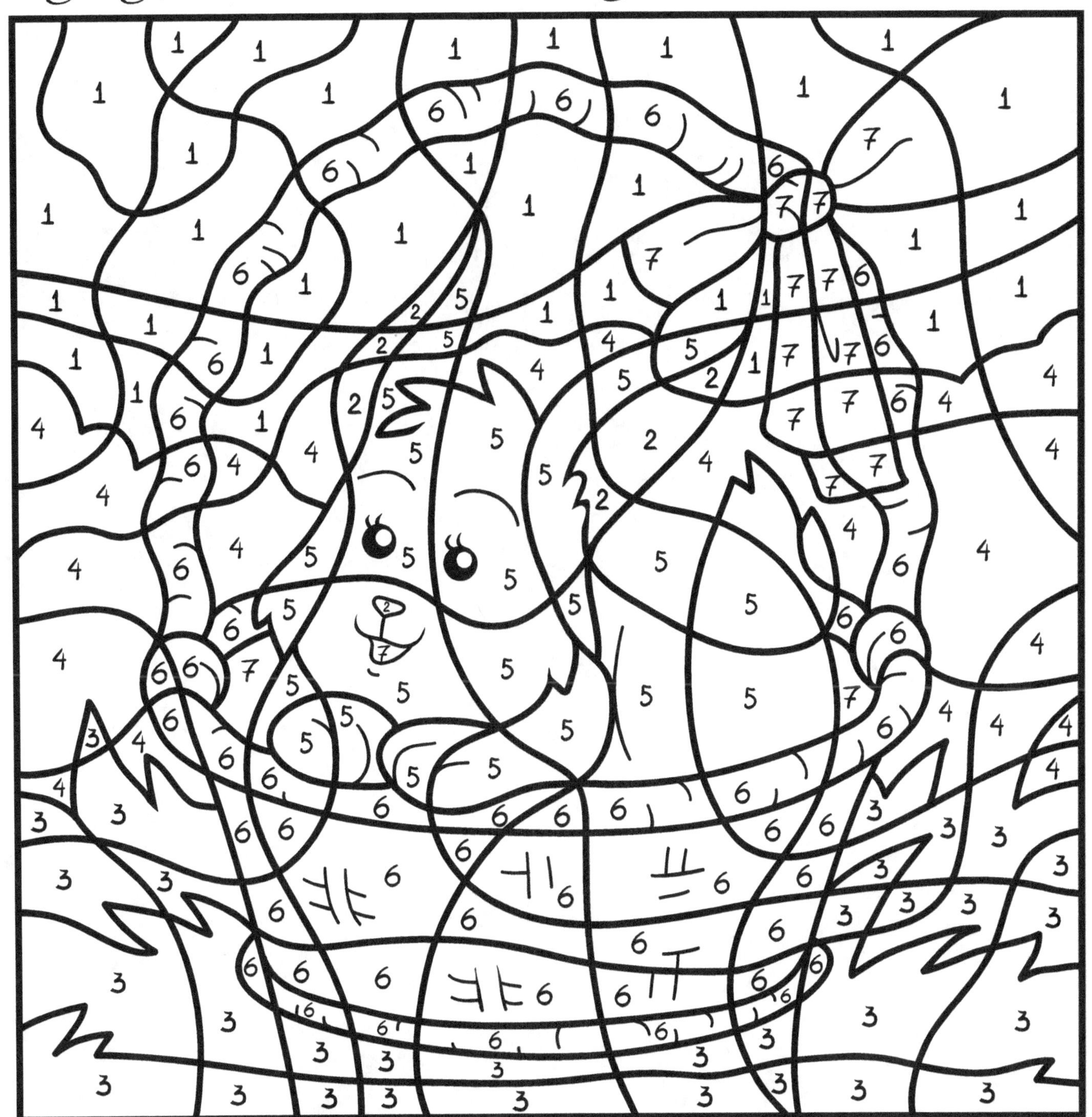

Draw and color a picture of the EASTER EGG using the grid.

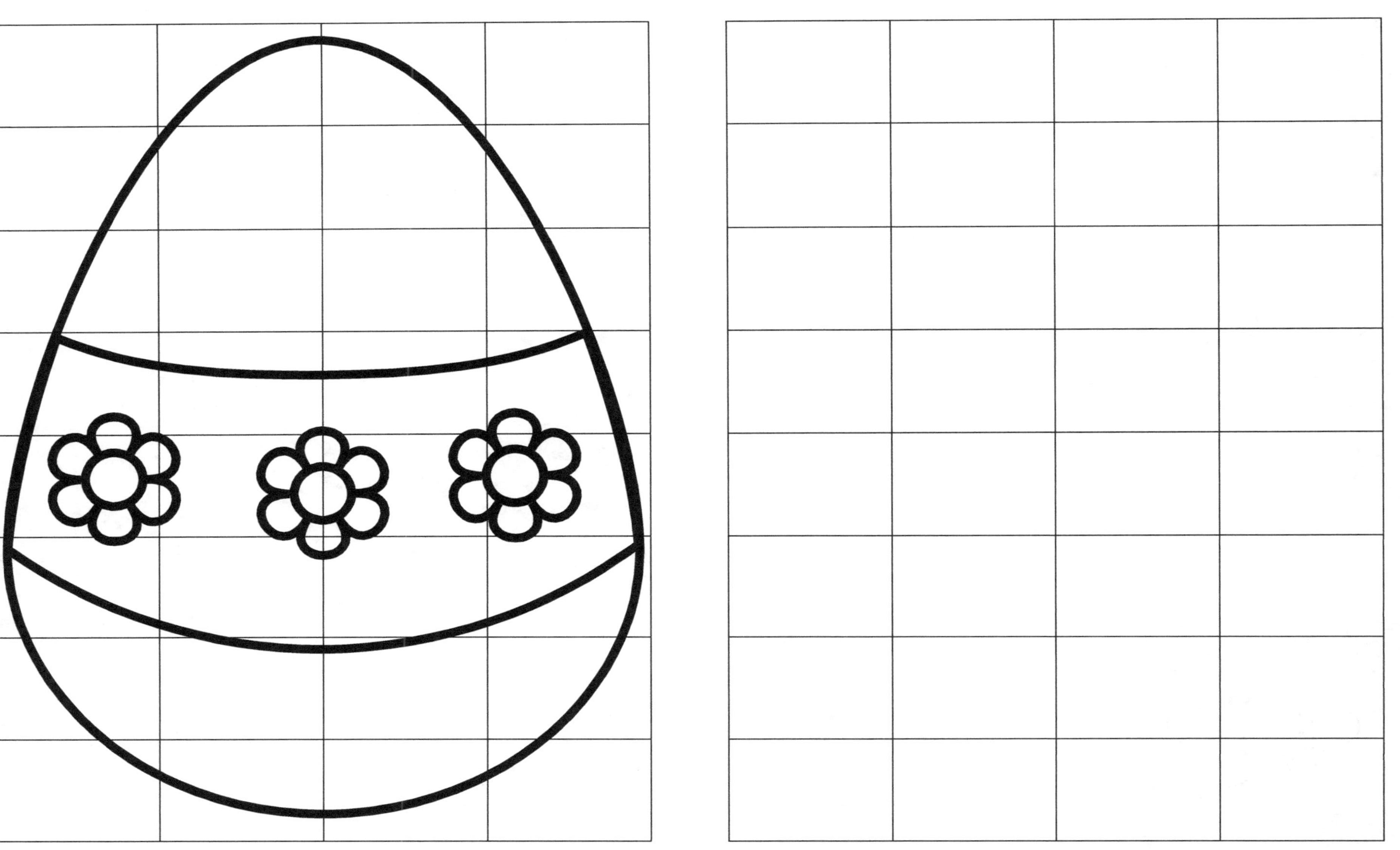

A FANTASTIC FRIEND'S Easter Egg Tree Maze

RABBIT'S CROSSWORD PUZZLE
Complete the puzzle and color the happy rabbit.

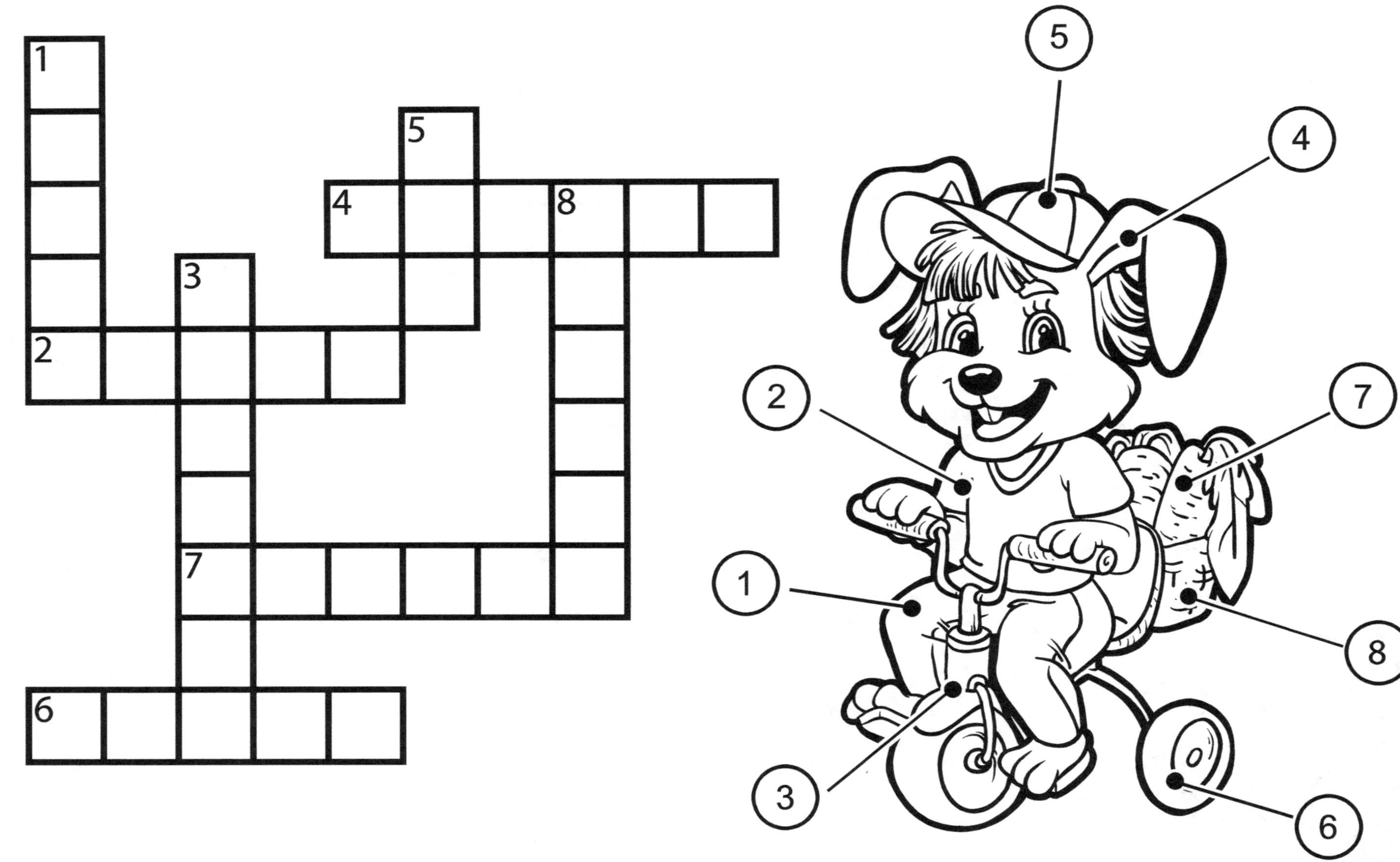

EASTER WORD GAME FOR MY FRIEND!

Write a word that begins with each of the letters from Happy Easter.

h_______________________________________

a_______________________________________

p_______________________________________

p_______________________________________

y_______________________________________

e_______________________________________

a_______________________________________

s_______________________________________

t_______________________________________

e_______________________________________

r_______________________________________

Use the letters at the bottom of the page to fill in the boxes. Then color the animals as you name them.

1 b _ _ r
2 b _ _ l
3 c _ _ k
4 f _ _ h
5 h _ _ e
6 i _ _ x
7 l _ _ n
8 w _ _ f
9 p _ _ y
10 s _ _ l

io   oc   ar   ul   is

be   ol   ea   on   ea

NUMBER EGG MAZE
Complete the mazes and color the eggs and frame. Which number reaches the EASTER EGG?

EASTER BUNNY DOT-TO-DOT!
Connect the dots and then color the FUNNY BUNNY.

EASTER ACTIVITIES FOR MY FANTASTIC FRIEND:
Crossword Puzzle, Word Search, Mazes, Poems, Songs, Coloring, & More!

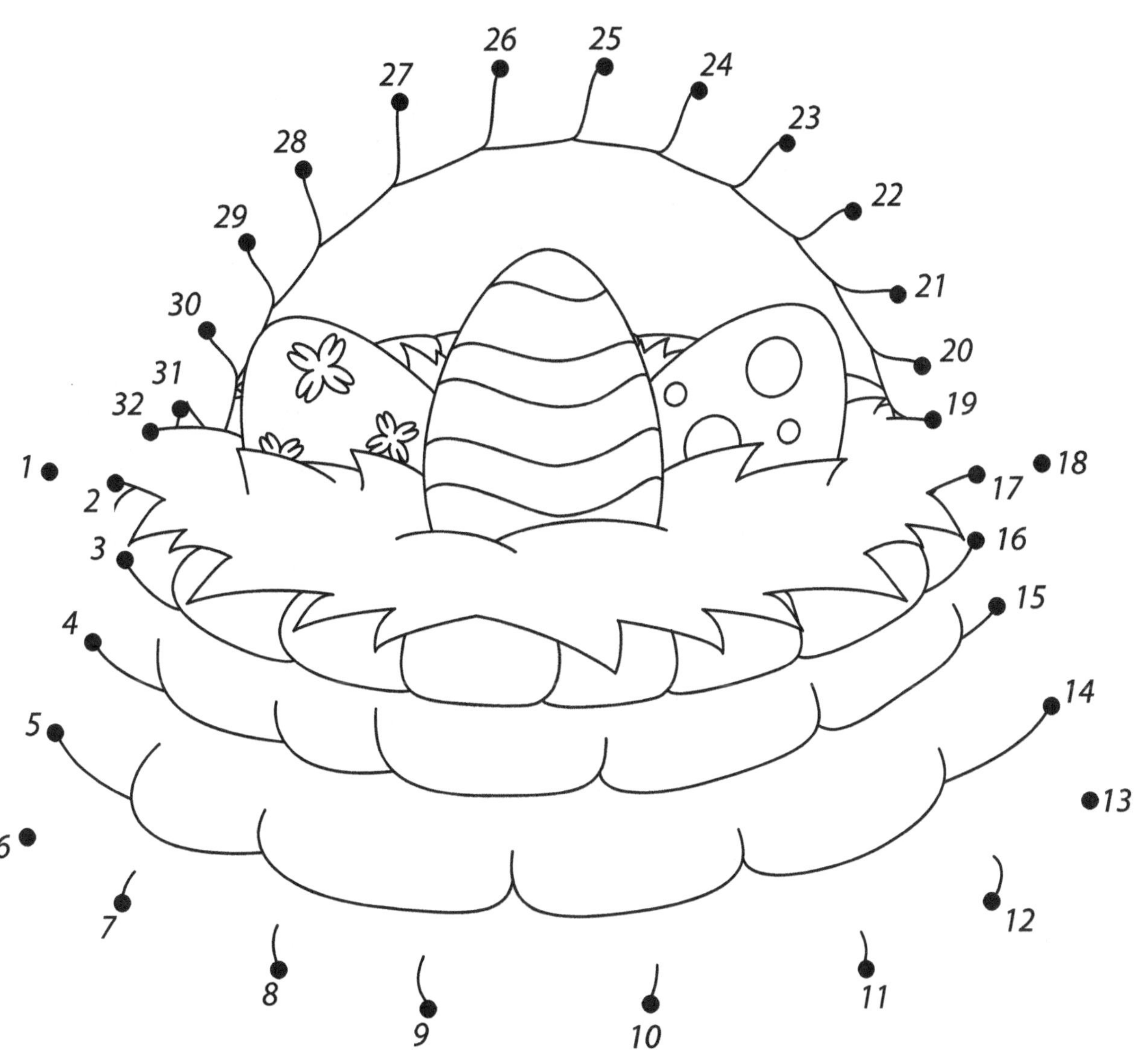

Connect the dots (from 1-32) and then color the
EASTER BASKET.

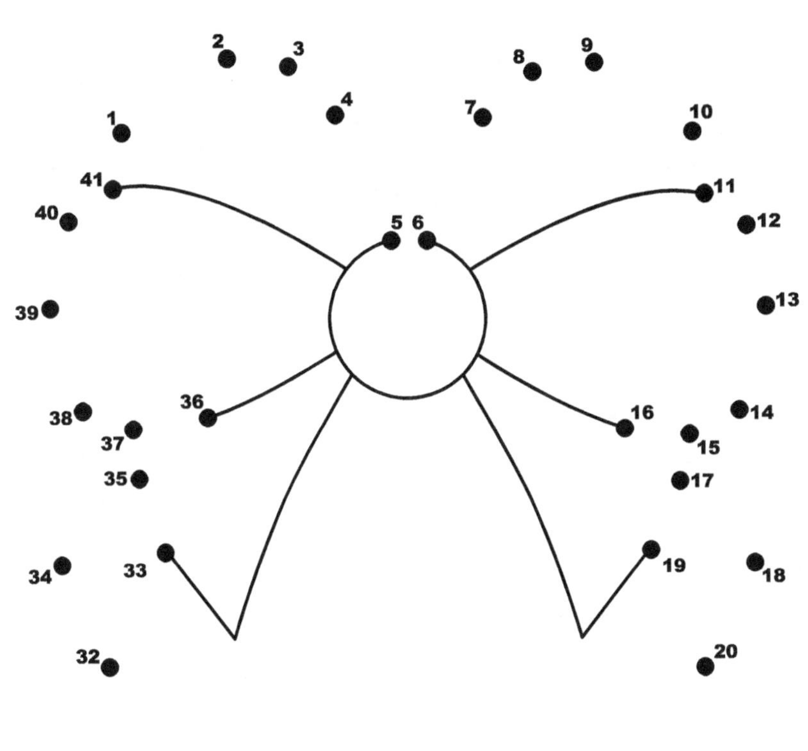

Connect the dots, color, and decorate the EGG.

We hope you've
enjoyed our fun-filled
EASTER ACTIVITY
BOOK
Happy Easter!
Florabella Publishing, LLC

HAPPY EASTER

www.ingramcontent.com/pod-product-compliance
Lightning Source LLC
Chambersburg PA
CBHW081847250726
48659CB00008B/2644